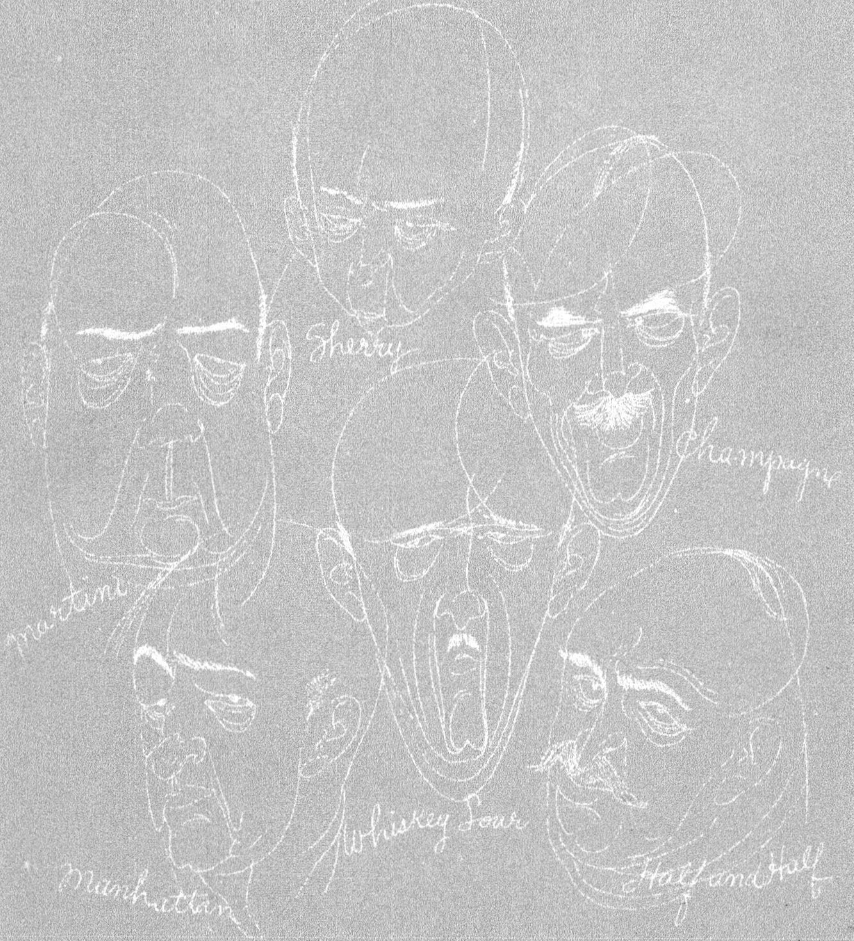
Sherry
Champagne
Martini
Whiskey Sour
Manhattan
Half and Half

HANGOVER

By ALEX KENNÉ

Introduction and Comments by Robert Gibson

FARRAR, STRAUS AND COMPANY · NEW YORK

Copyright 1948 by Alex Kenné
All rights reserved

First edition Gauleux Publishing Company, Inc., 1948
Second edition Farrar Straus and Company, 1949
Third edition Hotchkiss Publishing, 2017

ISBN: 978-0-9909020-6-5

Printed in the United States of America

HOTCHKISS PUBLISHING
17 Frank Street
Branford, CT 06405
email: bill@hotchkisspublishing.com
www.HotchkissPublishing.com

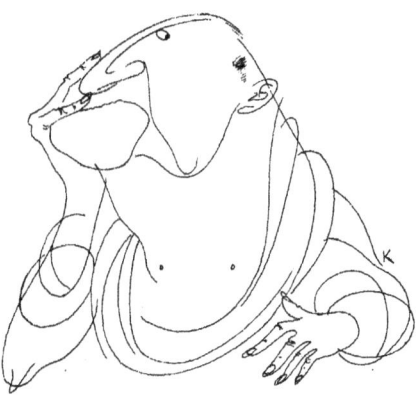

THE PURPOSE OF THIS BOOK is neither to disturb nor interfere with a well and honorably established custom. Today, the welcome opening of a friendly door is automatically followed by the opening of a bottle. This action of good cheer is firmly founded. Since, from the earliest recorded knowledge of man, he is discovered seeking means of subjectively increasing his sense of well being. Such pursuit of happiness, however, may produce a curious and unwanted by-product, the hangover.

The phenomenon of the hangover appears to have been either slighted or deliberately by-passed by artists, contemporary as well as ancient. Weavers of medieval tapestries seem to have preferred unicorns to pink elephants. The hangovers of history, which during Roman times alone must have been fabulous in scope, have gone their wavering way unrecorded and doubtless unlamented. We search in vain for one drawing of Cleopatra's legions of personal maids concocting eastern herbs to treat the after effects of the royal binge upon the royal barge. And we can find no picture of one of the wives of Henry VIII attempting to cure the kingly headache before her own poor head rolled into the waiting basket.

Alex Kenné by exploring and giving artistic recognition to the hangover, takes you into a world separate and apart. Upon entering this somewhat trackless region it may be observed that his pen occasionally traces a schizophrenic line. The method and style have direct relation to his subject, for it is a subject uniquely enriched by a variety of sensations. Floating upon the surface of an uncertain sea may give way to a plunge into helpless hilarity or borderline hysteria. In confused combination the hangover assumes overlapping shapes of phantasy, subconsciousness and unreality which may be heightened by physical or mental distress.

To enter the world of the hangover and feel no pain has heretofore been virtually impossible. By providing passport into a territory previously accessible only to those holding a ticket found in a bottle, this book now makes such an excursion possible. Since we do not frown upon that ticket, the following suggestion may not be unwelcome. Should it be in the quiet of the early evening that you first find this book between your hands, lay it aside momentarily. Take up the ingredients in the order named. To two thirds (*or more*) of gin add one third (*or less*) of dry vermouth. Stir with cautious care around a piece of ice and gently pour the glittering liquid into a glass chilled to tomb temperature. An olive is not recommended as it takes up too much space in the glass. Baptise with oil from the twist of lemon peel. Drink . . . fortified thus, or by any other means close at hand, you are better prepared to enter the wonder world of the hangover.

Here's looking at you!

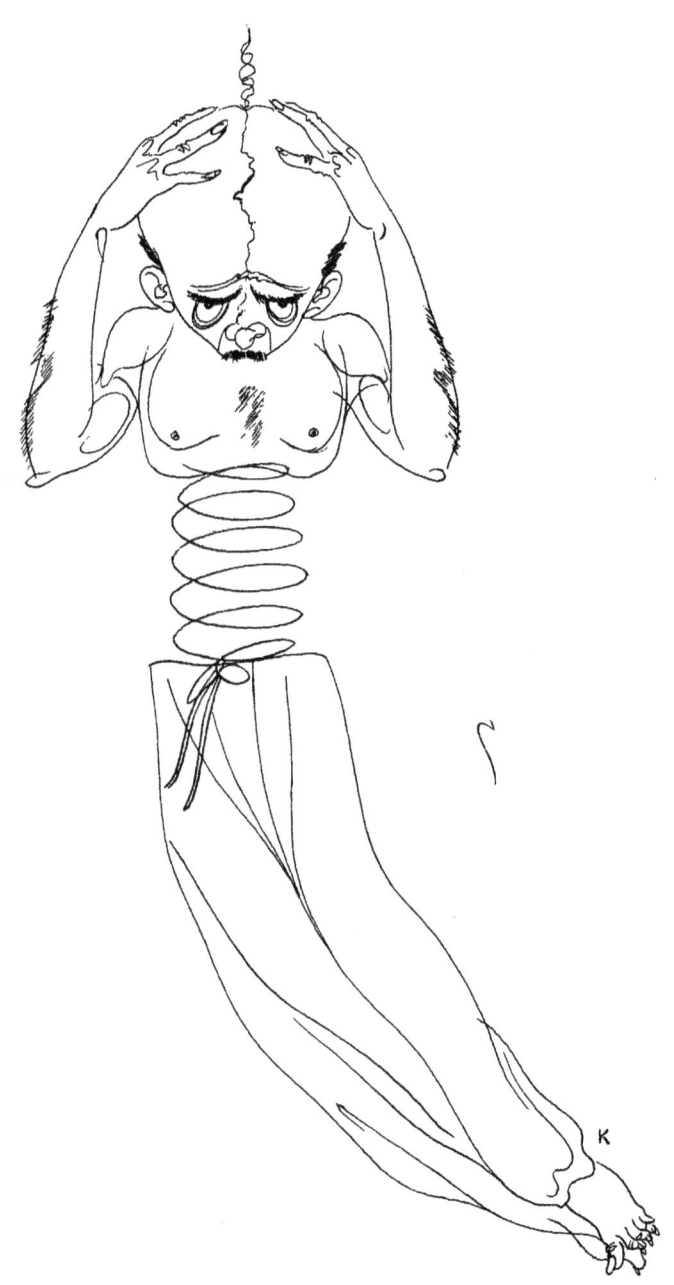

You whirl into space from your lonely bed

An amphibious ride is something to dread

Seconds seem hours in the course of your trip

While things go past at one hell of a clip.

Cold Comfort

A wistful pal you found in the night

Is a strange bedfellow by dawn's early light

Torment persists beneath your skin

Irrespective of the room you're in

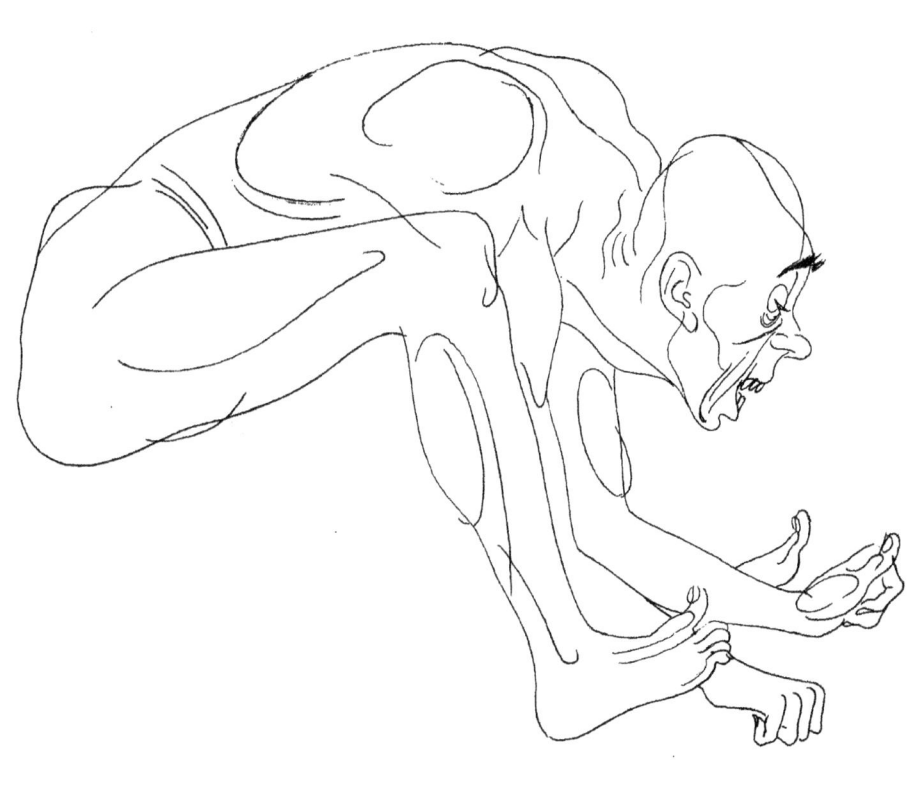

Visiting Hour

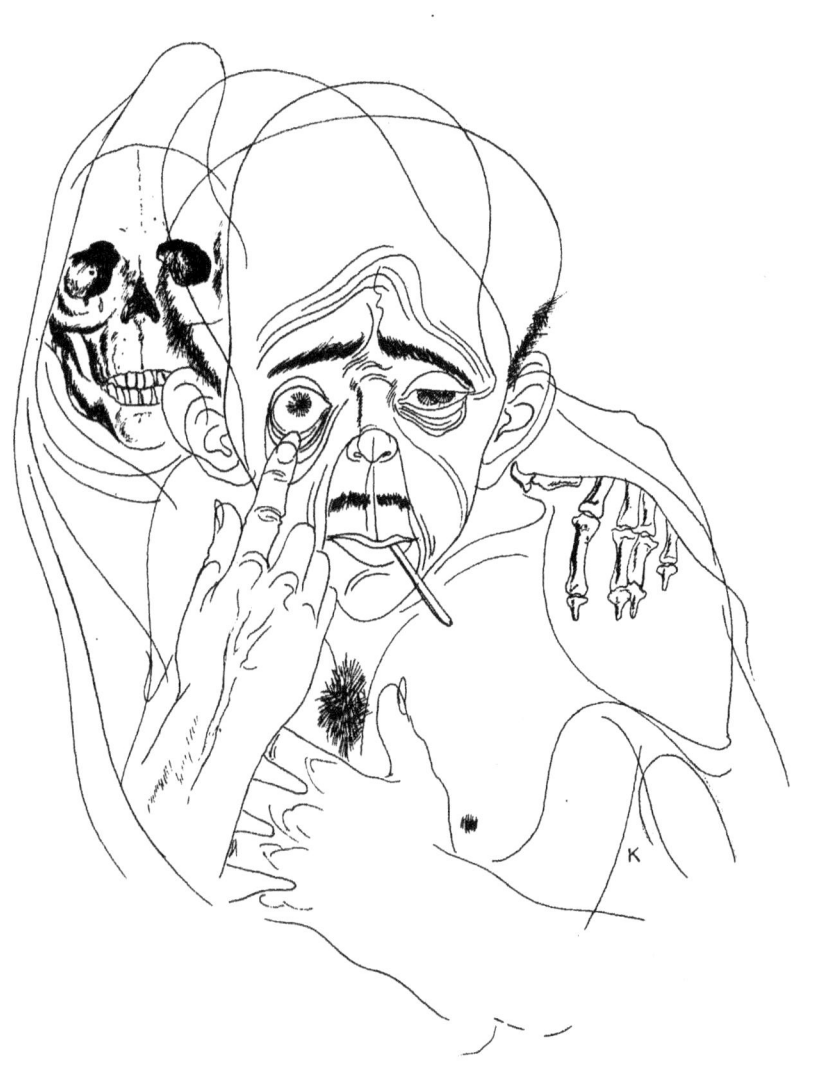

Uncertain memory filled with dread

Guiltily clings to your worried head

Dehydration

Fancy food and drinks recalling

Starts your stomach rising —— falling

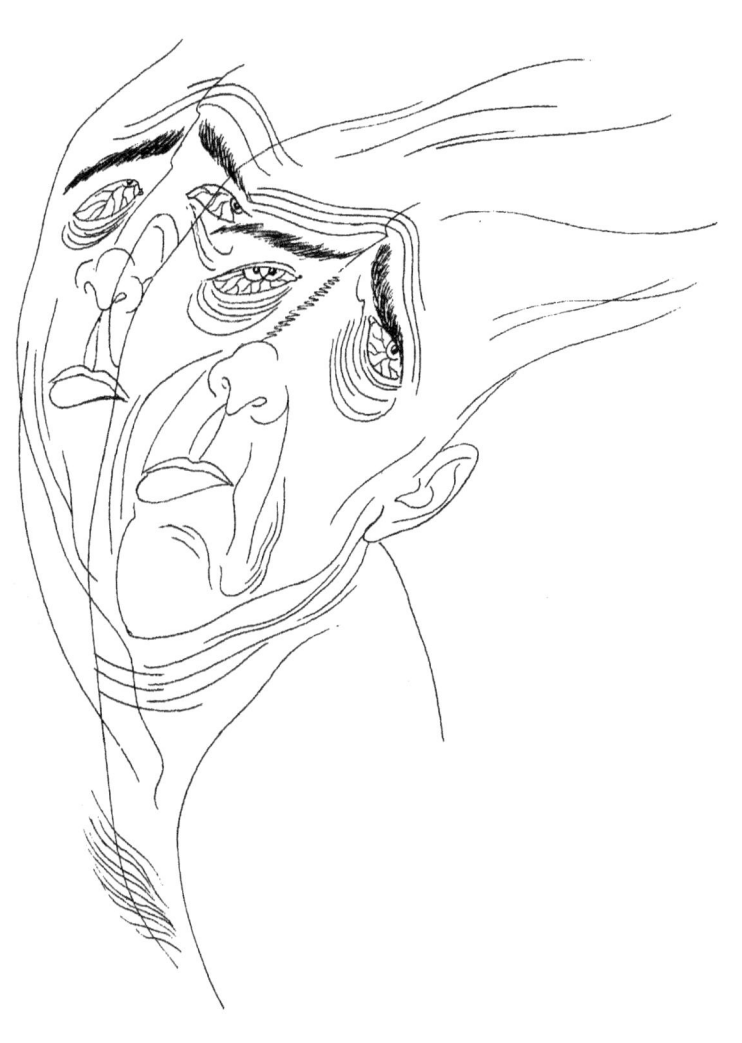

Turn the latch

On the nasty batch

Storm Impending

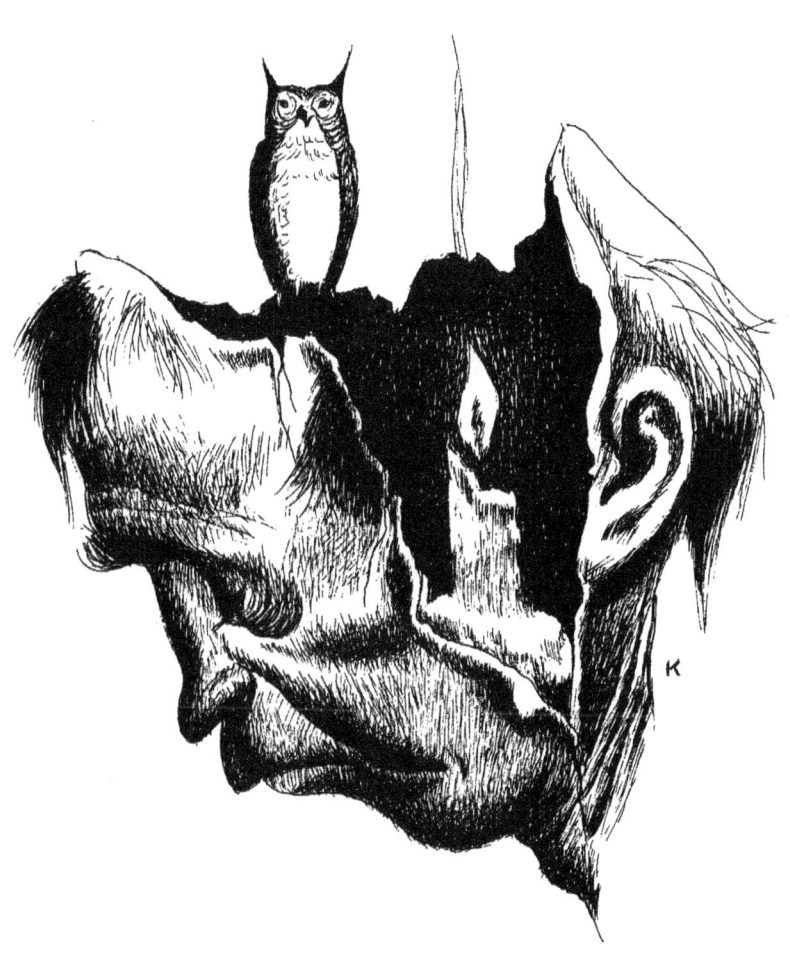

Strife Unending

Safely secreted within the shower,

Neither wanted nor loved

for the next long hour,

Unwilling to stand—unable to sit,

You sneak a hair of the dog that bit

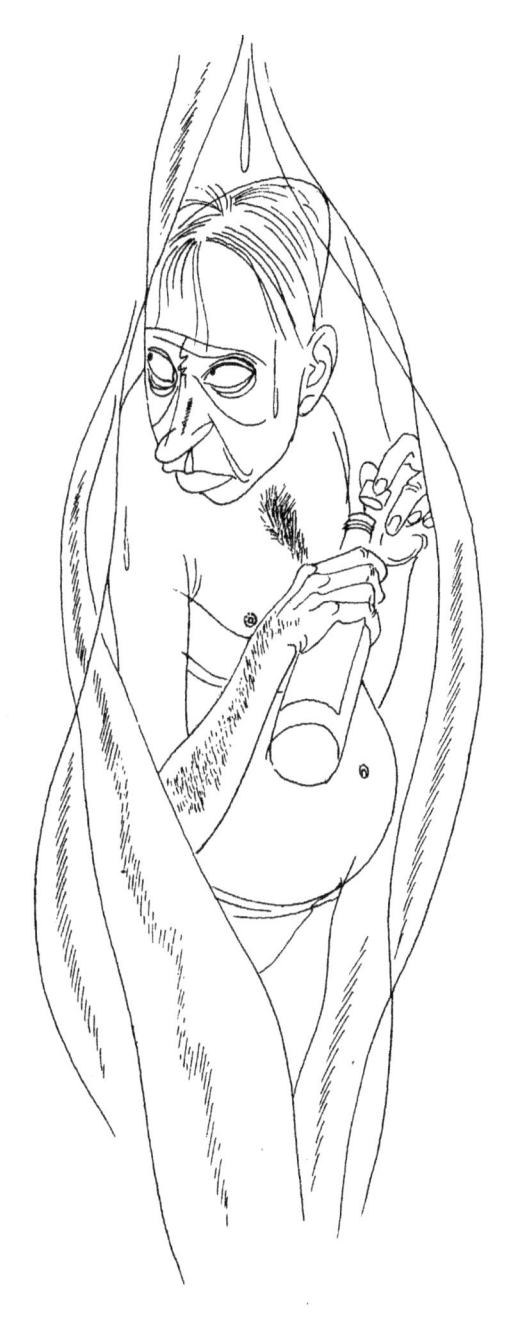

Straighten uppers are hard to choose

More of the same—you blow a fuse

You're better off not using force

So — just let nature take its course

You look with murderous intent

Upon the pigeons pleasure bent

Underslung and overshot

Blind take off

Now . . .

you've been through it

    Let's get to it

ABOUT THIS BOOK

"Before the publication of this volume it was virtually impossible to enter the realm of the hangover without considerable pain. By providing a passport into a territory previously accessible only to those holding a ticket found in a bottle, this book makes such an excursion possible. The publishers suggest you send copies to your friends before they play a similar trick on you. This a book that is more blessed to give than receive."

—*From the original dust jacket.*

ABOUT THE ARTIST

Alex B. Kenné
March 3, 1904 - August 11, 1977

New York native and longtime resident of Millbrook, NY. Mr. Kenné attended the Art Students League, New York City and the Julian Academy, in Paris. He was best known for his sculpture, paintings, and as a draftsman. He also illustrated a number of children's books. He found his subjects by looking to "mankind and his environment. The physical aspect of man as well as his psychic and spiritual counterpart." His style ran the gambit from classic landscapes to abstract as well as somewhere in between. He chose to use varies art forms because doing so offered "means of expression of changing the medium. Some things lend themselves to sculpture almost immediately. "

HOTCHKISS PUBLISHING
17 Frank Street
Branford, CT 06405
email: bill@hotchkisspublishing.com
www.HotchkissPublishing.com

ALSO AVAILABLE FROM HOTCHKISS PUBLISHING

The Sandy Beach Collection

DEAR FRIEND
Letters for Your Spiritual Journey, Volumes 1 & II

Soon after Sandy retired to Tampa he took advantage of his new schedule to write a number of meditations. We have collected 52 of them in Volume I which was published for his 50th anniversary December 7th 2014, Pearl Harbor Day. In each of the books Sandy shares some of the humble wisdom he has developed along his spiritual journey. Dear Friend provides a wonderful format as a personal guide or as a basis for weekly group meetings.

Volume I: Weekly spiritual meditations, each reading offers an accompanying page for journaling.

Volume II: Presents the remainder of Sandy's Dear Friend writings for your continued meditations and journaling.

STEPS AND STORIES
History, Steps, and Spirituality of Alcoholics Anonymous

Sandy considered this talk to be his quintessential work and we are sure you will agree. He recounts the remarkable confluences of people that lead up to Bill W. and Dr. Bob first meeting in Akron and tells little known stories from early AA history and along the way. Did you know that during the first Canadian convention in Montreal the nearby Seagram's Distillery flew its flags at half-mast, or how the Serenity Prayer came into use with AA? Sandy's perspective on the Steps makes clear from Step One that you are beginning a spiritual journey. His "slide projector" provides wonderful imagery and clarity to Steps 4 through 12. Sandy offers a message of hope in a way which makes the steps accessible to all and spirituality a desirable goal.

BOTTOMS UP
A Recovery
by Paul C.

Adams, Mass native and Melbourne resident Paul C. was an accomplished journalist and photographer. He created this book, his third, as a legacy. Through a series of engaging vignettes Paul tells his "story" from his perspective of 37 years in recovery from alcoholism. Paul passed away in May 2016, having just completed Bottoms Up.

Boiler Maker   Brandy

Bay Rum   Rye and water   Side Car